Sept. 13, 1980

Dear Laura & Julie,

We hope your visit was an enjoyable one. When you come again we will see more of Boston.

Love,
Sandy & Jerry

A BOSTON
PICTURE BOOK

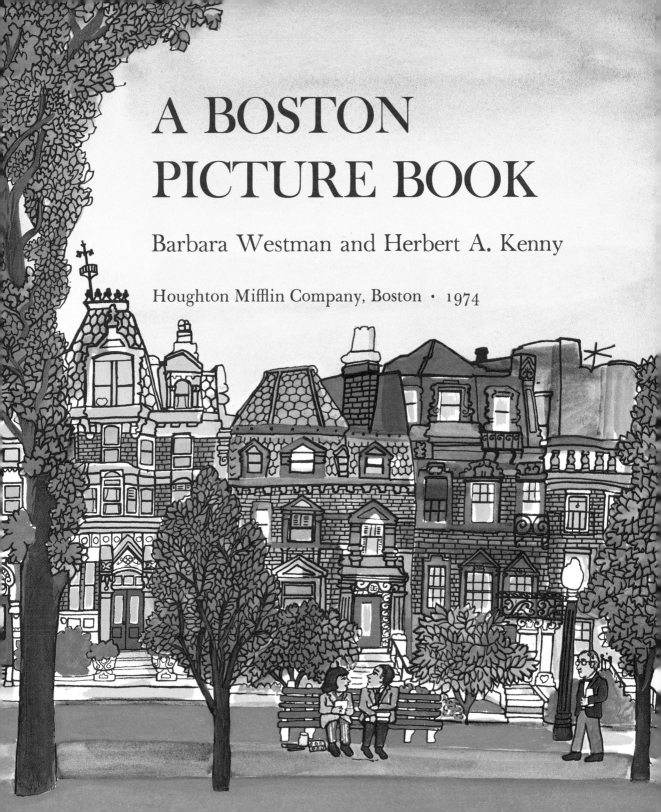

A BOSTON
PICTURE BOOK

Barbara Westman and Herbert A. Kenny

Houghton Mifflin Company, Boston · 1974

First Printing   H

Library of Congress Cataloging in Publication Data

Westman, Barbara.
  A Boston picture book.

  1. Boston—Decription—1951–   —Views.
I. Kenny, Herbert A., joint author.   II. Title.
F73.37.W47   917.44′61′0440222   74–3079
ISBN 0–395–19336–2

Printed in the United States of America

Reader, remember, the story of man
began in a garden; Boston's can
likewise. So, let us take our start
in the Public Garden, the city's heart.
Stand on the bridge, a few yards wide
and 100 feet from side to side
which spans the water, and watch below
a lazy pontooned vessel go
with a stern like a swan and a man astride
who peddles so passengers may ride
as leisurely as potentates
while it circumnavigates
the tiny island and contoured pond
back to childhood and dreams beyond.
These are the swanboats and, if you please,
nothing is purer Bostonese.

Beyond the pond and tulip beds
eight noble statues rear their heads,
men cast in bronze and turning green,
with elms and oak trees in between.
George Washington upon his horse
would lead us westward on our course
but we turn east where the Common calls
thousands to its lawns and malls,
to stroll or hurry, sit or sprawl,
play tennis, Frisbee or baseball —
the public's since sixteen thirty-four
and sure to be ours a few years more.

In the sun with a song and a soft guitar
Young people sit on the Common grass.
What a contented court they are,
In the sun with a song and a soft guitar
As they sing to their hearts, "Make love not war!"
How we wish we could stay, as the swift years pass,
In the sun with a song and a soft guitar.
Young people sit on the Common grass.

Barbara Westman

Now the tempo quickens
Along Charles street.
The crowd of shoppers thickens.
In festive mood they greet
Each other in this neighborhood
With its muted hippy beat.

If a hungry patron needs a
Sandwich or fried scrod,
He'll find it here . . . or pizza?
Tony's got it. Odd
That antiques mix with launderettes,
The stuffy with the mod?

Not in Charles Street madding
Where centuries collide,
Gas lamps and boutiques adding
Charm to the local pride
While bombazine and denim
Go shopping side by side.

Lampposts line Mt. Vernon Street,
Golden fruit on iron trees,
Classic doorways, purpled glass,
Gracious Georgian courtesies,
Paneled doors and polished brass,
Miniature lawns with miniature grass,
An ambiance that aims to please.

Satyrs dance on Beacon Hill!
So I've heard a native say.
Evenings when the wind is still
Satyrs dance on Beacon Hill,
Hooves on cobbles, piping shrill.
Nights in a wilder, wanton way
Satyrs dance on Beacon Hill.
So I've heard a native say.

Mount the hill, the pavement boasts
Antique bricks, the houses ghosts,
Iron footscrapes, hitching posts.
    The gardens lie behind.

Here Longfellow wooed his wife,
Copley cleaned his palette knife,
Motley wrote some Dutchman's life,
    And the late George Apley dined.

MT. VERNON ST.

Barbara Westman

The Bar Association's here,
The Athenæum's very near,
A library whose atmosphere,
   Is terribly refined.

Here's the seat of Government,
Of the Unitarian dissent
Near the Robert Gould Shaw monument
   Where brotherhood's enshrined.

Above, the State House rears its golden dome
In legislative dignity and peers
Down Park Street where the usages of years
Make the façades familiar as your home.

From Brimstone Corner to the Union Club,
Minister, publisher, priest and broker brush
Banker and politician who may rub
More than their shoulders in the noonday crush.

Westman

In and out of the kiosks on the run
Commuters dart in ant-like divagations.
The Hare Krishna neophytes' gyrations
Clash with the tempo of the carillon.

While on the Common where a fountain showers,
Young lovers with their backs to all of this
Dream of a Camelot and jeweled towers,
And, leaning into the future, bend and kiss.

What used to be the City Hall
Now is a café, bank and all.
You stop and stare and gazing at you
Is Benjamin Franklin, that is, his statue.
One of Josiah Quincy, too.
(He was a famous mayor, that's who.)
The building smacks of the Tuileries
And to the left where you see the trees
King's Chapel broods and some famous graves
Of decent folk and a brace of knaves.
Speaking of knaves, this City Hall knew
A lot of them — well, one or two.

Leave it there with its mansard charm.
Below is a shop that will disarm
The weariest traveler with its store
Of anecdote and lit'ry lore:
The first Old Corner Bookstore where
Emerson had his favorite chair,
Hawthorne browsed and Holmes penned notes.

If we had time for anecdotes
We'd cross the street to pause and browse
In the hallowed Old South Meeting House
Where the raucous Sons of Liberty
Decided to dump King George's tea.

We're off to honor the sacred dead
Where the first American blood was shed.

"Oh, Attucks was a Negro
And Carr from an Irish clan,
But until their blood
Mixed in English mud,
No blood was American."

For we have come to State Street
And the Old State House.
Here the Boston Massacre
Spurred a revolution.
Here Washington the statesman
Confirmed the new republic.
Bostonians remember:
Today men march in cadence
With military banners
And drum and fife and bugle
In proud commemoration
To Faneuil Hall, the cradle
Of liberty and the nation.

Let's move back toward Beacon Hill.
See that kettle! Big as a still!
If you wonder how much fills
That kettle, try a pint, three gills,
And, oh, one thousand and ten quarts,
Or so the manager reports.
But never mind, push on, let's enter
The Grand Piazza of Government Center.
What a magnificent sweep of stone,
With ruddy brick to set the tone
And tune the towers and stairs and all
To the antique charm of Faneuil Hall.

How well the new weds to the old!
This City Hall is something bold,
Asserting its varied symmetries
With robust grace. It stands at ease,
Linking at least three centuries.

Now let's descend to Union Street
Where once sea captains came to eat
So close to the sea they could smell the salt
Mix with the fumes of their wine or malt.
For the harbor stood where the markets stand
So much of the city is filled-in land.

Signs, signs, signs, signs
With funny words and strange designs,
Signs beckoning, signs curious,
Signs minatory and furious,
Signs that cajole, signs that deplore,
Signs that say less, signs that say more,
Signs square, octagonal and round,
Signs in the sky and signs on the ground,
Signs for sale, and signs for sales,
Small as ants and big as whales,
Signs in tandem, signs at random,
Signs till you cannot hardly stand 'em!
For now our winding, wandering pace
Has led to Boston's market place.

Shop! Then beyond the highway's bend
See the glorious North End.

If ever your elder daughter marries
For dowry take her to Polcari's
And let her buy to her heart's content
Every confetti and condiment —
Italian coffee and ronzoni,
Tamarind syrup, macaroni,
Cinnamon sticks and olive oil,
Sesame seeds, and before they spoil,
The ripest peppers, kidney beans,
And dozens of cheeses — beyond your means.
For dinner take her to Felicia's
With its consummate Italian dishes.
Enjoy our Little Italy
As European as can be.
The North End is its Boston name,
But it's Little Italy all the same.

One if By Land

Two if By Sea

Historic? Yes, it's very old.
The story has been often told
Of the Old North Church and the signals hung
In the days when the colony was young.
Hanover Street leads to the sea
Past some patchwork history.
St. Stephen's Church helped win respect
For Bulfinch, our first architect.
The Old North Church is so historic
Its signal lights are metaphoric —
They lit the birth night of a nation.
The legend still gives inspiration.
A small park called the Prado here
Boasts a statue of Paul Revere,
While many a patriot has found
Peace in Copp's Hill Burying Ground.
From there you gaze down on the sea,
Munificence and mystery.

Sailboats nod in the docks, a snowy spanker
Luffs on a yawl, while tugboats and a tanker,
Power boats, draggers nestle at the piers.
People have been sitting here for years
Placid as granite, regular as the tides.
There, where the harbor pilot schooner rides,
The airport buzzes with a thousand planes
Rising above the crisscrossed arms of cranes.
A handsome yacht glides by. A little later
We read the ensign of a foreign freighter.
Warships are not far off and never were:
Old Ironsides or an aircraft carrier.
This is the Boston waterfront, a port,
Sanctified by history, a fort
For a nation, and for the refugee
A gateway to a shining destiny.

It's late now and we turn back to the river.
The moon's on an early rise. We sense a shiver
In the ocean breeze. Come, look across the black,
Silver, slow-paced waters. Lost years back
That agitated patriot Revere
Rowed from this shore, not very far from here,
And shaped, like silver in his crafty hand,
The destiny of his father's new-found land.
Beyond our dimming sight, veiled in the dark,
An obelisk of granite crowns a park,
Commemorates a battle, men who cried
"Liberty!" and fought for it, and died,
Those men who gave their lives on Bunker Hill,
Whose legacy is courage, strength of will.
For Boston is a city where the past
Speaks to the future and the good things last.

45

Reader, before the evening shadows harden
To night, we wend back to the Public Garden.
There's so much more to Boston than we've shown —
Go in good health to find it on your own.